TABLE OF CONTENTS

Page

TABLE OF CONTENTS... i

ACRONYMS iii

CHAPTER 1 INTRODUCTION 1

    The Problem.. 1
    Primary Research Question 3
    Secondary Research Questions... 3
    Key Terms... 4
    Limitations 5
    Significance of this Research.. 5
    Background 6
    Chapter Summary 8

CHAPTER 2 LITERATURE REVIEW 10

    Category One: Literature On and Causes of a Problem.. 10
    Category Two: Literature that Defines Toxic Leadership and Identifies
    Characteristics.. 18
    Category Three: Toxic Leadership Solutions 19
    Chapter Summary 21

CHAPTER 3 RESEARCH METHODOLOGY 25

    Research Method 25
    Research Design 26
    Secondary Research Methodologies.. 27
    Ethical Considerations 29
    Research Planned But Not Executed 29
    Chapter Summary 30

CHAPTER 4 ANALYSIS 32

What is the Definition of Toxic Leadership?.. 32
What are the Specific Characteristics of Toxic Leadership? 37
Do Toxic Leadership Characteristics Have a Gender Component to Them?.............. 41
What Can be Done to Effectively Identify, Address and Reduce
Toxic Leadership?... 44
Chapter Summary 48

CHAPTER 5 CONCLUSIONS AND RECOMMENDATIONS 51

Conclusions.. 51
Recommendations.. 51
Chapter Summary 53

APPENDIX A ORAL HISTORY QUESTIONS 54

APPENDIX B CONSENT AND USE AGREEMENT FOR ORAL HISTORY
MATERIALS...61

APPENDIX C INTERVIEW WITH CSM TERESA KING 63

BIBLIOGRAPHY...67

ACRONYMS

ADP	Army Doctrine Publication
ADRP	Army Doctrinal Reference Publication
AR	Army Regulation
BG	Brigadier General
CAPT	Captain (O-6), Navy
CPT	Captain (O-3), Army
COL	Colonel (O-6)
DA	Department of the Army
DoD	Department of Defense
FM	Field Manual
GEN	General (O-10)
LTC	Lieutenant Colonel (O-5)
MAJ	Major (O-4)
OER	Officer Evaluation Report

CHAPTER 1

INTRODUCTION

The Problem

There are no bad regiments, only bad colonels.
— Napoleon Bonaparte in Farwell, *Encyclopedia of 19th Century Land Warfare: An Illustrated World View*

There are good leaders and notoriously bad leaders. As far back as the Civil War, the leadership of General Ulysses S. Grant is legendary. A fellow general once said General Grant's truly greatest qualities were "his innate modesty, his freedom from every trace of vain-glory or ostentation, his magnanimity in victory, his genuine sympathy for his brave and sensitive foemen, and his inflexible resolve."[1] The actions of General George Armstrong Custer, for example his indifference to his troops, placed him high on the list of a top 10 worst military leaders.[2] The experienced Fleet Admiral Chester Nimitz, who was selected to accept the surrender of the Japanese to close World War II, was well liked. As a result of not "cleaning house" upon his assumption of command of the Pacific Fleet, Admiral Nimitz endeared himself to his new staff, and they worked tirelessly for him.[3]

Lieutenant General Norman Schwarzkopf was a household name in 1991 during Operation Desert Storm. He embodied his personal philosophy that "character, competence, selfless service, and really caring about people were the cornerstones of a great leader."[4] Perhaps it is still too early to declare definitive historically successful and failed leaders of our current conflicts, Operation Enduring Freedom and Operation New Dawn, but the likes of Lieutenant Colonel Nathan Sassaman, who deliberately defied

1

Army values with his appalling decisions to cover up the illegal behavior of this unit during Operation Iraqi Freedom, are present in today's ranks. To this day Lieutenant Colonel Sasserman tries to defend his decision to order the leaders of his Battalion 6-7 Infantry Command in Iraq to intentionally lie to investigators about their involvement of the possible death of an Iraqi detainee.

General George S. Patton had a meteoric rise to military fame, yet it is doubtful in today's armed forces that the career of any officer could survive slapping a soldier in the face. "In 1943, Lieutenant General Patton slapped a soldier who was hospitalized for psychoneurosis, accused the soldier of cowardice and ordered him back to the field."[5] Times have changed. Or have they? The heroics of good leaders and their positive behaviors need not be questioned. What can be questioned is how to catalog the bad behavior or unfavorable characteristics. Does time and the operational environment change what is acceptable behavior? An enormous change since World War II is the advancement of women into higher levels of military leadership positions.

Napoleon Bonaparte placed blame for the poor performance of units squarely on the shoulders of his colonels. He makes an inference to the fact that it is the leader that makes a difference in an organization.[6] Dialogue on poor leadership in today's military is being discussed in terms of toxicity. The challenge for most service members today is trying to define toxic leadership. Everyone knows it when they see it, but few can define it. Additionally, there has not been a glossary definition in any official military Department of Defense (DoD) reference or publication. There are multiple subjective definitions of toxic leadership. Army Doctrinal Reference Publication (ADRP) 6-22, *Army Leadership,* published in August of 2012, defines toxic leadership as "a combination of self-centered attributes, motivations and behaviors that have adverse effects on subordinates, the organization and mission performance."[7] This definition has not been out in the field long enough for any scrutiny.

There is a cultural crisis in the Armed Forces in regard to toxic leadership. Hardly a published issue goes by between the *Army Times* and the *Navy Times* that a leader is not relieved of his or her duties due to toxic leadership. Many leaders being removed are female. One has to wonder what actions and behaviors the female leaders are exhibiting to be labeled toxic. Is there a gender component in toxic leadership? I argue that the concept of toxic leadership has an untheorized and neglected gender component.

Primary Research Question

According to the "U.S. Department of Defense, Selected Manual Statistics, Annual, and Unpublished Data Report," there were a total of 205,500 active duty women in the military as of 30 September 2010. Of that total, 38,700 women were officers and 166,800 were enlisted.[8] Approximately14 percent of the military are females. Since toxic leadership is on the rise and increasingly being reported, the primary research question becomes: Is there a gender component to toxic leadership?

Secondary Research Questions

In order to address the primary question, several other questions need to be answered. The first step towards a conclusion about toxic leadership is to define it. Toxic leadership must be defined to establish a baseline with a common understanding by all. My research questions include: what is the definition of toxic leadership? Once toxic leadership is defined, the follow up questions are:

1. What are the specific characteristics of toxic leadership?

2. Do these characteristics have a gender component to them?

3. What can be done to effectively identify, address and reduce toxic leadership?

4. Once a leader has been identified or labeled as toxic, can he or she be rehabilitated?

5. Are there leadership styles that can be promoted to combat toxic leadership?

6. Are the senior leaders of the military sending a clear message that they are not going to tolerate toxic leadership?

Key Terms

To better understand toxic leadership as it applies to the subject of "leadership," a few words are defined. The lack of an official DoD definition of toxic leadership is discussed in chapter 4. These words are used throughout the research paper and are key terms used in government and military leadership communities when discussing leadership. The definitions of the words are derived from military doctrine and published documents from civilian and military institutes.

Army Leader: Anyone who by virtue of assumed role or assigned responsibility inspires and influences people to accomplish organizational goals.[9]

Attributes: Characteristics unique to an individual that moderates how well learning and performance occur.[10]

Command: The authority that commanders in military service lawfully exercise over subordinates by virtue of rank or assignment.[11]

Culture: The set of longheld values, beliefs, expectations, and practices shared by a group that signifies what is important and influences how an organization operates.[12]

Leadership: The process of influencing people by providing purpose, direction, and motivation, while operating to accomplish the mission and improve the organization.[13]

Profession of Arms: The vocation to all whose work involves mastery of the discipline and open, collective application of force in pursuit of public purposes.[14]

Self Awareness: Being aware of oneself, including one's traits, feelings and behavior.[15]

Limitations

This research applies to leaders of all branches of service in the United States (U.S.) Armed Forces, but will heavily emphasize U.S. Army perspectives and policies. The research is focused on battalion level commanders, command sergeant majors and above. The scope of the research is from January 2003 to August 2012. Studies from around the world are used in this research thesis. DoD Civilians are not explicitly being addressed in this research paper. It is however understood that DoD civilians are also leaders of formations within DoD. I acknowledge that they can also contribute to both the toxicity of an environment or combatting the toxicity in an environment.

My contribution is principally theoretical. In order to confirm that toxic leadership has an untheorized, neglected gender component, more empirical research including surveys and case studies is required.

Significance of this Research

We must renew our commitment to the Profession of Arms. We're not a profession simply because we say we're a profession. We must continue to learn,

5

to understand, and to promote the knowledge, skills, attributes, and behaviors that define us as a profession.[16]

General Martin E. Dempsey said it best in his "Letter to the Force" once he assumed his role as the 18th Chairman of the Joint Chiefs of Staff.[17] All too often one just assumes that we know what is going on with a topic and no academic rigor is applied to the matter. Perhaps General Dempsey was giving credence to the current operational environment as a possible reason for poor leadership. The Army is in a prolonged state of transition. This era is fragile and filled with challenges and uncertainty. Resources are limited and acquisition questionable.

This thesis is an attempt to understand and acquire objective knowledge on the matter of toxic leadership. Leaders portray definite behaviors that affect organizations. When those behaviors are incompatible with good order and discipline or promote an incorrigible environment, members of the profession of arms must act quickly to identify and address the behaviors. An assumption by the field is that it is difficult to clearly identify what is toxic leadership. As a result, female leaders are getting falsely labeled toxic for exhibiting traditionally male characteristic. Awareness, identification, reporting and education, are steps to correct an unacceptable climate and preventing it from developing in the first place, or in the future. Additionally, we can change the completely gender neutral manner in which leadership is taught, and how leaders are professionally developed to adapt to ever changing environments.

Background

Within the last five years, all services in the U.S. military have seen a spike in what is being called "toxic leadership." In recent public reports, brigade level commanders, command sergeant majors and other senior leaders were relieved of their commands because of "toxic leadership." Toxic Leadership is often the "red-herring"[18] to describe a poor command climate or loss for confidence in a commander. Out of the currently known reports of toxic leaders, several are female.

There are several subjective definitions of toxic leadership. The term toxic leadership is now engrained in the lexicon of conscientious organizations across the military. The Air Force, Navy and Marine Corps reference a definition by Dr. George E. Reed (Colonel, Retired). In his 2004 article titled "Toxic Leadership" for the *Military Review.* He said "toxic leadership, like leadership in general, is more easily described than defined, but terms like self-aggrandizing, petty, abusive, indifferent to unit climate, and interpersonally malicious seem to capture the concept."[19]

Female leaders, both commissioned and non-commissioned officers, are possibly inadvertently being labeled as toxic leaders and are being removed from their positions. The term toxic leader is an ill-defined label for which service members are being reprimanded.

Organizations cannot be efficient or effective in an operational environment if toxicity is present. Women have been serving in the military since the Revolutionary War in 1775, and as of 2009, they make up 13.3 percent of all field grades (O-4/Major) and above positions. The Armed Forces has struggled for over 237 years to figure out how to precisely deal with women in the ranks, and slapping a label on female leaders is the latest attempt at course correction to improve leadership. When a leader is "toxic," it further throws off the balance or equilibrium for an organization, and this can degrade a unit's morale.

Albert Einstein said "setting an example is not the main means of influencing another, it is the only means."[20] If the services are going to be serious about curbing toxic leadership, then the field needs to see examples of toxic leaders in order to make dealing with toxic leaders more tangible and fixable.

Chapter Summary

There is a history of poor leadership in the Armed Forces. Perhaps the current toxic trend is due to the operational environment. With no definition to start with, one can never get the term "toxic leadership" out of the realm of a passing fad and to be taken seriously. Senior leaders have charged the force with addressing the issue of toxic leadership. The fragile state of the military cannot afford the effects of toxic leaders. Toxic leaders are no longer favored in today's Armed Forces.

Awareness of a problem is the first step to solving problems. Addressing the true definition and clarification of toxic leadership and its proper application can clean up the battlefield in the battle of the sexes and provide some clarity, predictability, stability and reliability in the leaders' commanding formations.

---

[1]The Ulysses S. Grant Homepage, http://www.granthomepage.com/grant general.htm (accessed 4 May 2012).

[2]TopTenz, "2012 Top 10 Lists," http://www.toptenz.net/top-10-worst-military-leaders-in-history.php (accessed 4 May 2012).

[3]2012 HubPages Inc., http://thejeffriestube.hubpages.com/hub/Admiral-Chester-Nimitz-Savior-of-the-Pacific-Fleet (accessed 4 May 2012).

[4]The American Academy of Achievement, http://www.achievement.org/autodoc/page/sch0int-5 (accessed 5 May 2012).

[5]Dulcinea Media, Inc., "On this Day," http://www.findingdulcinea.com/news/on-this-day/July-August-08/On-this-Day--General-Patton-Shocks-Public-by-Slapping-Crying-Soldier.html (accessed 4 May 2012).

[6]Napoleon Bonaparte, Quoted in Byron Farwell. *Encyclopedia of 19th Century Land Warfare: An Illustrated World View* (New York, NY: W. W. Norton & Company, 2001).

[7]Headquarters, Department of the Army, Army Doctrine Reference Publication (ADRP) 6-22, *Army Leadership* (Washington, DC: Government Printing Office, August 2012), 3.

[8]U.S. Census Bureau, Newsroom, "Women's History Month: March 2012," http://www.census.gov/newsroom/releases/archives/facts_for_features_special_editions/cb12-ff05.html (accessed 29 June 2012).

[9]Headquarters, Department of the Army Field Manual (FM) 6-22, *Army Leadership* (Washington, DC: Government Printing Office, 12 October 2006), G3.

[10]Ibid.

[11]Ibid.

[12]Ibid.

[13]Ibid.

[14]Ibid.

[15]Ibid.

[16]General Martin E. Dempsey, "Letter to the Force," DoD Live.mil, 1 October 2011, http://www.dodlive.mil/index.php/2011/10/general-dempseys-letter-to-the-joint-force/ (accessed 22 July 2012).

[17]Ibid.

[18]Dr. Jon J. Fallesen, interview with author, Ft. Leavenworth, KS, 30 October 2012.

[19]COL George E. Reed, "Toxic Leadership," *Military Review* (November-December 2010): 58.

[20]Iain Hay, "Transformational Leadership: Characteristics and Criticisms," School of Geography, Population and Environmental Management, Flinders University, http://www.leadingtoday.org/weleadinlearning/transformationalleadership.htm (accessed 4 September 2012).

CHAPTER 2

LITERATURE REVIEW

There is a plethora of literature on toxic leadership. A June 2012 Google search of "military toxic leadership" yielded 118,000,000 results. However, there is a lack of literature on the specific topic of "female toxic leadership." A Google search of "female toxic leaders" yielded 5,140,000 results, mostly centered or registering on "toxic" and "leadership" and with the majority of references concentrating on the chemical component of the word toxic. The topic of toxic leadership is addressed primarily in gender neutral generalities.

In this chapter, the literature reveals its significance to the research topic. The literature provided is divided into three categories:

1. Category One: Literature and causes of a problem.

2. Category Two: Literature that defines toxic leadership and identifies characteristics.

3. Category Three: Toxic leadership solutions.

Category One: Literature On and Causes of a Problem

In order to reach an answer to question one: is there a gender component in toxic leadership?, research was conducted to find out if there really is a problem with toxic leadership in the military and what some of the causes are.

In the July 2011 *Army Times*, Walter Ulmer (Lieutenant General, Retired), a former III Corps Commander "estimates roughly 8 percent to 12 percent of Army officers at the rank of colonel and higher are so toxic that they need to be removed from command."[1] The magnitude of Lieutenant General Ulmer's statement is that the Army has approximately 64,502 officers,[2] leaving as many as 7,741 toxic officers within the ranks. Lieutenant General Ulmer has credibility because he commanded over 55,000 personnel at one point in his career, but it is his long standing contributions to the revival of ethical military leadership that have branded him an authority on leadership. In 1986, Lieutenant General Ulmer was instrumental in using the Mai Lei incident as an example of why the Army needs to work on ethical principles in the military.

A concrete, tangible, living example of a female leader being visibly labeled a toxic leader is found with Sergeant Major (SGM) Teresa King. In an October 2012 *Army Times* article written by Joe Gould, SGM King was accused and charged with fostering and condoning a "toxic" workplace environment, characterized by disparate treatment, insubordination to a superior, retaliation and low morale."[3] The article continues to quote SGM King's lawyer James E. Smith who ascertains that "as an assertive leader; [SGM King] was judged more harshly than a man would have been . . . There are different standards for a female in charge when it comes to toxic leadership, and the Army has a systematic issue with that."[4]

A journal article, "Army Leader Development and Leadership, Views from the Field," written by Ryan M. Hines and John P. Steele, Ph.D., discusses the results of the 2010 Center for Army Leadership (CAL) *Annual Survey of Army Leadership (CASAL).* With the participation of 22,500 Army respondents, this report provides both qualitative and quantitative data. Based on *CASAL* data points, one leader in five is viewed negatively for: (1) not putting unit needs ahead of his own (22 percent), (2) being 'a real jerk" (25percent), (3) doing things and behaving in a way that is negative for the organization, himself, and subordinates.[5]

Captain George J. Athanasopouos's article in the *Army Magazine* asserts "inadequate development of leaders is a cause of toxic leadership."[6] It also lists specifics that the Department of the Army is implementing to attempt to tackle toxic leaders. For example, the Multi-Source Assessment Feedback (MSAF) of which a 360-degree evaluation is a requirement. The 360-degree Evaluation is an assessment tool where an officer can get feedback from the officer himself/herself, three superiors, five peers and five subordinates.[7] It has not been fielded for the Non-commissioned Officer (NCO) Corps at this time.

"The Quick Wins Paradox," by Mark E. Van Buren and Todd Safferstone lists five signs to watch to identify a toxic leader:[8]

1. Focuses too heavily on the details.

2. Reacts negatively to criticism.

3. Intimidates others.

4. Jumps to hasty conclusions.

5. Micromanages direct reports.

Bruce Heller, in his review"Toxic Boss Syndrome, What Are the Causes and Cures?" states that: "Toxic bosses are emotional bullies who treat employees coldly, even cruelly. They assign blame and take the credit for themselves." Heller also states that 80 percent of toxic bosses can be rehabilitated if they change their personality.[9]

George E. Reed (Colonel, Retired), a former faculty member from CAL, writes extensively on toxic leadership. In "Toxic Leadership,"[10] he describes three elements of what he calls "toxic leader syndrome:"

1. An apparent lack of concern for the wellbeing of subordinates.

2. A personality or interpersonal technique that negatively affects organizational climate.

3. A conviction by subordinates that the leader is motivated primarily by self-interest.

Reed also states that it is not just one specific behavior that deems one toxic; it is the cumulative effect of demotivational behaviors on unit moral and climate over time that tells the tale.[11] In "Toxic Leadership, Part Deux," Reed references a Harvard Professor's spin on "bad leadership" that includes incompetent, ridged, intemperate, callous, corrupt, insular and evil.[12]

The civilian sector also struggles with toxic leaders but they are labeled as bad leaders, toxic bosses or mangers and even extreme descriptions such as corporate psychopaths. In a 1991 study, Dr. Robert D. Hare, a world renowned authority on psychopaths identifies cooperate psychopaths as:

> being glib and superficially charming, with a grandiose sense of self-worth, as being pathological liars who are good at conning and manipulating others, have no remorse about harming others, and are emotionally shallow, calculating, cold, callous and lacking in empathy and that they are people who fail to take responsibility for their own actions.[13]

Contrary to toxic leaders, good bosses demonstrate a degree of earnest resolve when faced with a task. Michael J. Kelly explains five key characteristics of the best bosses in his article "Don't be a Bosshole:"

1. Grit.

2. The right amount of assertiveness.

3. A focus on small wins.

4. Awareness of how others perceive them.

5. A willingness to support and stand up for their people.

Kelly also writes about the need for a realistic assessment or a good mirror when it comes to evaluating ourselves as bosses. A major component in addressing toxic leadership is the leader's ability to see him or herself.

In the book, *Risky Business*, Lynne Falkin McClure Ph.D., identifies toxic behaviors in mangers, and the types of organizational cultures that foster the behavior. Dr. McClure is the President of McClure Associates Management Consultants, Inc. since 1980, and she specializes in work relationships for corporations and government agencies.[14] Dr. McClure asserts that "where your culture is and where your managers are is a first step in detoxifying a work environment."[15]

In 2011 the *Leadership Quarterly International Journal of Political Social and Behavioral Science* published "An Exploration of Stereotypical beliefs about leadership styles: Is Transformational Leadership a Route to Women's Promotion." The study predicts that descriptive stereotypes about sex differences in leadership style are substantially accurate and similar to assessments of real male and female mangers on specific behavior.[16] The study (depicted in table 2) concludes that descriptive gender stereotypes about leadership styles are accurate. "Participants with considerable management experience believe that women display more transformational and contingent reward behaviors, and fewer management-by-exception and laissez-faire behaviors than men."[17]

In the business sector, Pulitzer Prize nominated Professor of Public Policy and Organizational Behavior at Claremont Graduate Univeristy, California, and co-founding director of the Insitute for Advanced Studies in Leadership, Jean Lipman-Blumen, addressed six psychological factors that make people seek leaders.[18] Lipman-Blumen asserts that these needs are what lure people to toxic leaders. The military is a super incubator for each of her factors:[19]

1. Our need for reassuring authority figures to fill our parent's shoes.

2. Our need for security and certainty, which prompts us to surrender freedom to achieve them.

3. Our need to feel chosen or special.

4. Our need for membership in the human community.

5. Our fears of ostracism, isolation and social death.

6. Our fear of personal powerlessness to challenge a bad leader.

A 1995 study by Chemers and Murphy found that "in leadership roles, gender stereotypes are particularly damaging for women because agentic, as opposed to communal, tendencies often are indispensable."[20]

Professors Alice Eagly and Steven Karau, have researched extensively on gender issues on the topic of leadership and published a study "Role Congruity Theory of Prejudice towards Female Leaders." The findings in their study suggest that there exists perceived incongruity between the female gender role and leadership roles that leads to two forms of prejudice: (1) perceiving women less favorably than men as potential occupants of leadership roles; and (2) evaluating behavior that fills the prescriptions of a leader role less favorably when it is enacted by a woman.[21] The study asserts that the

17

consequences of the prejudices are: (1) attitudes that are less favorable towards female leaders than male leaders; and (2) it is more difficult for women to become leaders and to achieve success in leadership positions.

A 2005 article in *The Guardian*, a British newspaper, describes "the "macho" culture in their training barracks is shared by female soldiers too, many of whom become obsessed with the need to trounce the boys. And despite their enthusiasm, "GI Janes" often become targets of abuse."[22]

Category Two: Literature that Defines Toxic Leadership and Identifies Characteristics

Field Manual (FM) 6-22, *Army Leadership,* October 2006, clearly defines "leadership as influencing people by providing purpose, motivation, and direction while operating to accomplish the mission and improve the organization."[23] The draft of Army Doctrine Publication (ADP) 6-22, *Army Leadership*, addresses toxic leadership under the category of applying influence, and comes close to defining toxic leadership as "a combination of self-centered attitudes, motivations and behaviors that have adverse effects on subordinates, the organization and mission performance."[24]

"Toxic Leadership: When Grand Illusions Masquerade as Noble Visions," is an article written by Jean Lipman-Blumen that provides a definition of toxic leaders. It defines toxic leaders as "those individuals who by dint of their destructive behaviors and dysfunctional personal qualities generate a serious and enduring poisonous effect on the individuals, families, organizations, communities, and even entire societies."[25]

Karlene M. Kerfoot's article on leadership, "Civility and the No Jerks Rule," defines toxic employees as "those who are rude, temperamental and abusive, spread

18

gossip, create factions, distort communications to their ends, and sabotage work processes, colleagues and mangers." [26]

In the book, *Toxic Leader, When Organizations Go Bad,* Marcia Lynn Whicker defines toxic leaders as "leaders that are maladjusted, malcontent and often malevolent, even malicious. They succeed by tearing down others. They glory in turn-protection, fighting, and controlling, rather than uplifting followers. Toxic leadership plummets productivity and applies brakes to organizational growth, causing progress to screech to a halt."[27]

Category Three: Toxic Leadership Solutions

MilitaryCorruption.com is a source used to acquire the names and a version of the stories on why commanders are relieved. This site is operated by retired military personel and has more the 20 million "unique page views" dealing with military corruption and cover-ups, making it the largest in the world.[28] This site covers the Army, Air Force, Navy, Coast Guard, and Marine Corps. As of July 2012, it was reported on this site that 12 Navy Commanders were relieved between January 2012 and August 2012.

MilitaryCorruption.com also published two feature posts on SGM Theresa King on her suspension as the first female leader of the Army Drill Sergeant School, and on her lawsuit against Major General Longo and Command Sergeant Major Calpena, her demand for reinstatement, and the Congressional probe of her treatment.[29]

The website for the Center for the Army Profession and Ethics (CAPE) hosts the "Army Profession Campaign Annual Report" for calendar year 2011. This report does not discuss toxic leadership outright, but it does speak to many of the characteristics that have become synonymous with describing toxic leaders.

19

The researcher interviewed commanders/ leaders that have been in the news and labeled toxic leaders. Two proposed interviewees are Colonel Dianna Roberson, former Commander of 45th Sustainment Brigade, Schofield Barracks, Hawaii, and Command Sergeant Major Theresa King, the first female commandant of the Army Drill Sergeants School at Fort Jackson, South Carolina.

The 2004 *Encyclopedia of Leadership,* vol. 2, defines "Gender Egalitarianism as the state or condition of minimizing gender role differences and promoting gender equity and equality." [30] This term can explain the condition that plagues how leadership is taugh in the military. It also can be summarized as generder neutral.

An Alice H. Eagly and Mary C. Johannesen-Schmidt study in 1990 found that in a more traditional setting, where the male stereotype was more dominant, gender differences between men and women are more pronounced. Another Eagly and Johannsen-Schmidt study found meta-analysitic results and concluded that when men leaders were compared to women leaders they were perceived as more transactional leaders; specifically that they avoid giving direction and changing the status quo when performance goals are being met. [31]

A study by Becker, Ayman and Korabik in 2002 brought to light one consideration for methodology when researching gender leadership issues. The perceptions being evaluated originate for the subordinates of the leader.[32] In order to answer the question of "are men and women behaving similarly or differently?" the answer may be contingent upon the eyes of the perceiver, who is influenced by his or her stereotypes, expectations, and the social norms to which they have been exposed.[33] In other words, if the male subordinate grew up believing that the military is no place for a woman, or that the proper place for a woman is at home raising children, then his perception of how his female military boss is performing will be skewed, most likely in a negative direction. However, if he grew up with a pioneering female role model who excelled in a traditionally male field, management for example, then his perceptions of his female boss would be less disagreeable.

In addressing the increase of women in leadership roles at the highest levels of organizations, in her study J. D. Yoder found that women leaders have found ways to lead that finesse the remaining incongruity between leader roles and the female gender role. Transformational leadership may be especially advantageous for female leaders because they do not elicit the resistance that women tend to encounter when they proceed with behavior more typical of men.[34]

In Spring 2003, *The Journal of Business and Psychology*, published a study by Barbara Mandell and Shilpa Pherwani entitled "Relationship between Emotional Intelligence and Transformational Leadership Style: A Gender Comparison." This study asserts that "there is a predictive relationship between transformational leadership style and emotional intelligence."[35]

Chapter Summary

There is an abundance of literature on toxic leadership and there are a multitude of different leadership techniques and styles for both men and women. Literature is lacking in thoroughly understanding and exploring the gender component in regards to how toxicity is developed, fostered and combatted between men and women. Enough evidence is available from the current literature to conclude that there is a distinction on how and why women are labeled as toxic leaders.

[1]Michelle Tan and Joe Gould, "Army Wants to Rid Top Ranks of Toxic Leaders," *Army Times*, 31 July 2011, http://www.armytimes.com/news/2011/07/army-wants-to-rid-ranks-of-toxic-commanders-073111w/ (accessed 10 July 2012).

[2]About.com, "US Military Promotions," http://usmilitary.about.com/od/promotions/l/blofficerprom.htm (accessed 17 June 2012).

[3]Joe Gould, "Circus of Mistakes," *Army Times,* 22 October 2012.

[4]Ibid.

[5]Dr. John P. Steele, *CASAL: Army Leaders' Perceptions of Army Leaders and Army Leadership Practices* (Ft. Leavenworth, KS: Center for Army Leadership, June 2011), 1.

[6]CPT George J. Athanasopouos, "Improving Toxic Leadership," *Army Magazine.*

[7]Tan and Gould.

[8]Mark E. Van Buren and Todd Safferstone, "The Quick Wins Paradox," *Harvard Business Review* (January 2009): 55, http://hbr.org/2009/01/the-quick-wins-paradox/ar/1 (accessed 12 June 2012).

[9]Bruce Heller, "Toxic Boss Syndrome, What are the Causes and Cures?" *Sales and Service Excellence* (June 2010): 15.

[10]Reed.

[11]Ibid.

[12]COL George E. Reed, "Toxic Leadership, Part Deux," *Military Review* (November 2010).

[13]Clive R. Boddy "Corporate Psychopaths, Bullying and Unfair Supervision in the Workplace," *Journal of Business Ethics* (2011): 367-379; Springer, "Ethical Leadership," *Journal of Business Ethics* (2009): 3.

[14]Dr. Lynn F. McClure, *Risky Business* (Binghamton, NY: Haworth, 1996), http://books.google.com/books?id=KUSUcetrUBQC&dq=Lynne+Mcclure+Risky+Busin ess&lr=&source=gbs_navlinks_s (accessed 6 June 2012).

[15]McClure.

[16]C. J. Vinkenburg, "An Exploration of Stereotypical Beliefs about Leadership Styles: Is Transformational Leadership a Route to Women's Promotion," *The Leadership*

Quarterly International Journal of Political Social and Behavioral Science, 22 (2011): 11.

[17]Ibid., 10.

[18]Jean Lipman-Blumen, *The Allure of Toxic Leaders* (New York, NY: Oxford University Press, 2005), 29.

[19]Ibid.

[20]Peter G. Northhouse, *Leadership; Theory and Practice* (India: Sage, 2011), 312.

[21]Alice H. Eagly, Steven J. Karau, and Mona G. Makhijani, abstract from "Gender and the Effectiveness of Leaders: A Meta-Analysis," *Psychological Bulletin* 117, no. 1 (1995): 125-145, http://www.ncbi.nlm.nih.gov/pubmed/12088246 (accessed 5 September 2012).

[22]Joanna Burke "From Surrey to Basra, Abuse is a Fact of British Army Life," *The Guardian*, 26 February 2005, http://www.guardian.co.uk/uk/2005/feb/26/military.iraq/print (accessed 29 August 2012).

[23]FM 6-22, G3.

[24]Headquarters, Department of the Army, Draft Army Doctrine Reference Publication (ADRP) 6-22, *Army Leadership* (Washington, DC: Government Printing Office, October 2011), 7-2.

[25]Jean Lipman-Blumen, "Toxic Leadership: When Grand Illusions Masquerade as Noble Visions," *Leader to Leader* (Spring 2005): 29.

[26]Karlene M. Kerfoot, "Leadership, Civility and the 'No Jerks' Rule," *Urologic Nursing* 28, no. 2 (April 2008): 149.

[27]Marcia L. Whicker, *Toxic Leaders; When Organizations Go Bad* (Westport, CT: Quorm Books, 1996), 11.

[28]MAJ Glenn MacDonald, USAR (RET), Editor-in-Chief, "Military Corruption," http://www.militarycorruption.com/ (accessed 5 September 2012).

[29]UK, "CSM Teresa King," http://www.militarycorruption.com/csmteresaking.htm (accessed 8 July 2012).

[30]George R. Goethals, Georgia J. Sorenson, and MacGregor Burns, *Encyclopedia of Leadership*, vol. 2 (Thousand Oaks, CA: Safe, 2004), 578.

[31]Ibid., 553.

[32]Ibid., 554.

[33]Ibid.

[34]J. D. Yoder, "Making Leadership Work More Effectively for Women," *Journal of Social Issues* 57, no. 5 (2001): 815-828.

[35]Barbara Mandell and Shilpa Pherwani, "Relationship Between Emotional Intelligence & Transformational Leadership Style," *Journal of Business and Psychology* 17, no. 3 (Spring 2003).

CHAPTER 3

RESEARCH METHODOLOGY

The purpose of this exploratory study is to identify a component in military leadership that can be attributed to female leaders becoming or being labeled toxic, compared to male leaders. The thesis seeks to ascertain if there are definitive factors that will cause women to be labeled toxic and what can be done about toxic leadership.

This chapter will present the research methods used to obtain the answers to the research questions. The questions that are being researched are: Is there a gender component in toxic leadership? (2) What is the definition of toxic leadership? (3) What can be done to effectively identify, address and reduce toxic leadership?

Research Method

Multiple methods are used to derive answers to the research questions. The researcher utilized qualitative and quantitative data to answer the thesis questions. Qualitative data seeks to provide an informed assertion on why and how the topic of research has come to be. Quantitative data refers to the systematic empirical investigation of social phenomena via statistical, mathematical or computational techniques.[1]

> The word empirical means information gained by experience, observation, or experiment. The central theme in scientific method is that all evidence must be empirical which means it is based on evidence. In scientific method the word "empirical" refers to the use of working hypothesis that can be tested using observation and experiment.[2]

Empirical data primarily from the "2011 Profession of Arms Survey" will determine if there is a problem. A review of different source materials was used to attempt to cover the full extent of challenges. The researcher examined publications from

25

CAL, primarily analyzing the results from the *CASAL* and the "2011 Profession of Arms Survey" conducted by CAPE. Additionally, a synopsis of "Army Leader Development and Leadership; Views from the Field" by Ryan M. Hinds and John P. Steel, Ph.D., will help determine the suitability, feasibility, and acceptability of the thesis.

Research Design

The quantitative Command and General Staff College Quality Assurance Office reviewed, approved and administered the surveys to several female leaders. Application and survey questions included in appendix A (surveys). A consent and use agreement for oral history was given to each interviewee (appendix B.) Interview questions which were posed to someone who was already labeled as a toxic leader were:

1. How would you advise future female officers to conduct themselves in order to avoid being perceived as a toxic leader?

2. Describe the specific characteristic or action(s) to be labeled a toxic leader?

3. What was your awareness of toxic leadership?

Members of CAL were consulted. For example, Colonel Thomas P. Guthrie, Director of CAL at Combined Arms Center-Leader Development & Education, provided direction and insight into what the Center was doing on the topic of Toxic Leadership. He allowed me to contact members of his staff. I consulted with a lead Combined Arms Center researcher, Dr. Melissa Wolfe, who provided instrumental source material and insight into the challenges with researching subjective topics in leadership and toxic leaders. She validated that the same list of toxic leaders that I was tracking were individuals that the Center was looking into. She recommendsedthat I meet with Dr. Jon Fallsen the Chief of the Leadership Research, Assessment and Doctrine Division in CAL.

26

This interview was invaluable and the discussion points are incorporated throughout the thesis.

Secondary Research Methodologies

To address the premise that the definition of toxic leadership is ill-defined, I argue that the current definitions are too subjective and measurable to be effective. Evidence of subjectivity can be found in the multiple definitions that exist.

A theoretical methodology was used to address the question, what is toxic leadership? The researcher used an article by Paul Staniland entitled "States, Insurgents, and Wartime Political Orders," as an example of the use of a theoretical methodology. In a theoretical methodology, the researcher gives examples or demonstrates the existence of their recommended theory, and seeks to develop their own recommendation to satisfy the conclusion of the subject being researched. The researcher provided suggested recommendations to redefine the term toxic leadership as well as reduce toxic leadership.

A tangible unit of measure was using case studies and people as a primary source of data. This study attempted to contact female leaders who have gone public or have a media spotlight under toxic leadership. This provided qualitative data in the form of first-hand knowledge, perspective, and further determination how this label affected the unit.

The study included reviewing the published works on adaptive leadership by leading pioneers in research such as Colonel John B. Richardson IV. The study also provided tangible acts, attitudes and examples of what not to do. The researcher theorizes that providing an example will be an effective approach to avoiding toxic leadership.

To address the premise that there is something going on with how and why female leaders are being labeled toxic, I argue that they are erroneously being labeled toxic for exhibiting masculine leadership traits. As evidence of this, I illustrate the situation of SGM Teresa King. By doing so a qualitative phenomenological research method was used. Phenomenological research is used to describe a "lived experience" of a phenomenon.[3] This research method seeks find out what happened to a subject, from the subject's unique perspective. It delves into finding out how the subject was affected, their emotions and observations. Phenomological research shows "what is," reality. In this research, the thesis question centers around the unique perspectives or phenomenon the female leaders in the case studies have experienced with being labeled toxic leaders in public forums. They are uniquely qualified to speak on their experiences and perceptions

To address the premise that gendered leadership is worthy of future inept study, I argue that there is not enough data being collected to effectively inform senior leaders that a modification in how leadership is taught is warranted. This is evidenced by the fact that the specifics of the reasons why or what specific actions or behiavior transpired to cause female leaders to be removed from their positions of leadership under the guise of being toxic. The additional research method employed was a plausibility probe. This method "involves probing the 'plausibility' of candidate-theories. Plausibility here means something more than a belief in potential validity, plain and simple; for hypotheses are unlikely to ever be formulated unless considered potentially valid; it also means something less than actual validity, for which rigorous testing is required."[4] SGM Teresa King is a plausible illustration of the veracity in the sentiment that female leaders are being labeled as toxic for exhibiting male characteristics. Another aspect of the plausibility probe is that it seeks to find out if the topic is worth further investment of resources to study.

28

Ethical Considerations

Ethical considerations made for this research consisted of safeguarding the data obtained from research subjects as well as the citing of the source of all external information. Care was taken in regards to the sensitivity of the subject matter for the human subjects. Their psychological wellbeing was a factor when considering the method of engaging with the human subjects. It was considered that the questions being asked and the subject matter could remind participants of traumatic events. A buffer was placed between the human subject and the researcher with the use of a written survey. This allowed the subject to obtain any desired legal assistance prior to submission in order to mitigate against self-incrimination.

Research Planned But Not Executed

The researcher planned to obtain data from the DoD Inspector General Office on actual number of official toxic leaders. Upon discussion with the DoD Inspector General Office, they could not provide actual numbers due to: (1) the privacy of the individuals; (2) the reality of ongoing investigations; (3) my lack of a substantial need-to-know; and (4) they did not have a neat and compiled database to query just female officers. The Chief of the DoD Inspector General could only validate the existence of the public cases, for example the case involving Colonel Dianna Roberson and SGM Teresa King.

The researcher planned to interview two other officers who were publically considered toxic and another who had unsubstantiated allegations of toxic leadership and was relieved of her command under the auspices of toxic leadership. Questions were compiled and approved by the Command and General Staff College Quality Assurance Office, for an interview with Colonel Dianna Roberson, but the researcher was unable to make positive contact with her. She is now retired and living a private life. Navy Captain

Holly Graf, a former Commander of the USS Cowpens was to be the other publicly

accused female. She was deemed to be too extreme and her behaviors were clear Uniform

Code of Military Justice offenses. The final officer who was to be interviewed, did

provide personal insights into the state of toxic environments during her time in

command, but declined to be included or published due to her retirement. Additionally,

under the tenets of a phenomonogical research method which allows for the proof of the

existence of the behavior or activity, the single contribution of SGM King who has been

publicly labeled as a toxic leader is scientifically sufficient to meet the burden of proof

for this research project. As an example, in a study called "The Lived Experience of

Postpartum Depression: A Phenomenological Study" by Cheryl T. Beck, the researcher

interviewed seven women who claimed to have postpartum depression based on certain

criteria such as experiencing the desire to hurt oneself or the baby.[5]

Chapter Summary

This chapter discussed the research methodology employed in the execution of

the thesis. This chapter discussed the executed and unexecuted data collection processes

of subject interviews and use of quantitative empirical data such as studies done by other

expert researchers in their respective fields of leadership and science. Combinations of

methodologies were employed, theoretical, phenomological and a plausibility probe, in

order to cover all bases and result in making a sound research paper.

---

[1]Lisa M. Given, *The Sage Encyclopedia of Qualitative Research Methods* (Los Angeles, CA: Sage Publications, 2008).

[2]Dr. Hani, "Empirical Research," Experiment Resources, 2009, http://www.experiment-resources.com/empirical-research.html (accessed 18 August 2012).

[3]Capilanou University, http://www2.capilanou.ca/programs/psychology/students/research/phenom.html (accessed 5 August 2012).

[4]University of California Press, http://publishing.cdlib.org/ucpressebooks/view?docId=ft0k40037v&chunk.id=d0e2943&toc.depth=100&brand=eschol (accessed 12 August 2012).

[5]Cheryl T. Beck, "They Lived Experience of Postpartum Depression: A Phenomenological Study," *Nursing Research* 41, no. 3 (May-June 1992): 166-170, http://psycnet.apa.org/psycinfo/1992-43176-001 (accessed 3 December 2012).

CHAPTER 4

ANALYSIS

> Performance that violates your values corrupts, and it will ultimately sap and destroy your strengths.
>
> —Peter Drucker,
> *Management Challenges for the 21st Century*

This chapter will group the secondary research questions and provide answers to them based on the collected literature from chapter 2. Following the answers to the secondary research questions, there is a qualitative analysis narrative on select integral documents. The secondary group research questions were:

1. What is the definition of toxic leadership?

2. What are the specific characteristics of toxic leadership?

3. Do these characteristics have a gender component to them?

4. What can be done to effectively identify, address and reduce toxic leadership?

Once answered, these secondary questions will lead to a final answer of the primary research question of: is there a gender component in toxic leadership? in the conclusion chapter.

What is the Definition of Toxic Leadership?

The definition of toxic leadership is still evolving. Toxic leadership is currently ill-defined and pejorative. Even senior leaders with over 30 years of service concur that there are problems with the term. According to SGM Teresa King "it is not well defined throughout the Army. Toxic Leadership must be defined at a level where all soldiers can understand it. It is routinely confused with leaders enforcing standards and used by subordinates to escape being held accountable."[1]

The most consistent discovery while attempting to define toxic leadership is that the definition is different for most personnel and it can be dependent upon a variety of sub-categories that one can belong to. Common sub-categories that can offer skewed perceptive are gender, branch of service, for example combat arms or combat service support, DoD civilian, or in the private sector. However, there are commonalities of characteristics that transcend all categories that can be agreed upon.

In August 2012, CAL published the first version of a definition in an official Army publication in ADP 6-22:

> Toxic Leadership is a combination of self-centered attributes, motivations and behaviors that have adverse effects on subordinates, the organization and mission performance.
>
> This leader lacks concern for others and the climate of the organization, which leads to short and long-term negative effects.
>
> The toxic leader operates with an inflated sense of self-worth and from acute self-interest. Toxic leaders consistently use dysfunctional behaviors to deceive, intimidate, coerce or unfairly punish others to get what they want for themselves.[2]

I have deconstructed the Army's definition and broken it down further into the three main categories and associated the stated characteristics in the category:

1. Self-Centered Attributes:

    a. Lacks concern

    b. Inflated sense of self-worth

    c. Acute self-interest

2. Motivations:

>   Get what they want

3. Behaviors:

    a. Deception

    b. Intimidation

    c. Coercion

    d. Unethical (unfair)

Of the three categories, behavior is the most tangible of the list. Behavior is an outward action that can be judged by others. It can be clearly observed and analyzed. A leader's behavior can be scrutinized and discussed and the leader can be held accountable for the behavior. It is possible that a behavior can be judged by others incorrectly, but an action can be adjudicated by peers and supervisors. One can get to a place of clarity on an action or specific behavior. It is much easier to get a person's motivation wrong. Unless a person specifically states his or her motivation, any attempt to categorize another person's motivation is pure speculation and will be a hypothesis. Much of the definition is focused on the intangible aspects of human behavior. Dr. Falssen of CAL did admit that the Center was aiming for a description of toxic leadership rather than a definition.

The private sector seems to be in the lead on research about unwanted behaviors from people in leadership positions, both male and female. With profit based motivations, poor leadership adversely affects the monetary bottom line for a business. In other words, most businesses cannot afford poor leadership.

"Toxic Leadership: When Grand Illusions Masquerade as Noble Visions," by Jean Lipman-Blumen that provides a definition of toxic leadership. It defines toxic leaders as "those individuals who by dint of their destructive behaviors and dysfunctional personal qualities generate a serious and enduring poisonous effect on individuals, families, organizations, communities, and even entire societies."[3] Karlene M. Kerfoot's article on leadership, "Civility and the No Jerks Rule," defines toxic employees as "those who are rude, temperamental, and abusive, spread gossip, create factions, distort communications to their ends, and sabotage work processes, colleagues and managers." [4] Both Lipman Blumen's and Kerfoot's definitions place great emphasis on the fact that a leader's negative behavior makes an indelible impact on a host of groups of people and institutions.

In the book, *Toxic Leader, When Organizations Go Bad*, Marcia Lynn Whicker defines toxic leaders as: "leaders that are maladjusted, malcontent and often malevolent, even malicious. They succeed by tearing down others. They glory in turn from protection, fighting, and controlling, rather than uplifting followers. Toxic leadership plummets productivity and applies brakes to organizational growth, causing progress to screech to a halt."[5]

Whitcker places a toxic leader more into the mental health categories similar to pathology. This is consistent with the notion of the medical tie of toxicity, diseased and detrimental to health, be it the health of the toxic leader him/herself, their followers or subordinates or their organization. Speaking of toxic leadership in terms of a disease or pathology is not uncommon in the military. According to Dr. Fallesen (General, Retired),

Ulmer also described toxic leadership as possible pathology—a character flaw that is engrained in some people.[6]

Bruce Heller, author of "Toxic Boss Syndrome, What are the Causes and Cures?" states that "toxic bosses are emotional bullies who treat employees coldly, even cruelly. They assign blame and take the credit for themselves." This definition places emphasis on the emotional component and how it registers with employees.

SGM King provided physical proof of toxic leadership in the ranks and had personal experience with toxic leaders: "My awareness of Toxic Leadership was leaders who were self-serving, who show and demonstrate a lack of concern for others, does not set the example, unethical, violated Army Values and UCMJ…. Yes I have experienced a toxic leader."

My recommendation for a definition of toxic leadership is: longstanding and emotionally abusive speech and behavior that have adverse effects on an organization. This makes the definition more objective and measurable. This also makes the message on toxic leadership easier to be received by the masses. It also separates toxic leadership from specific Unified Code of Military Justice violations. Physical abuse is clearly a violation and punishable by law. Verbal and emotional abuse is not. Verbal and emotional abuse can be charged under the Uniformed C ode of Military Article for conduct unbecoming of an officer or maltreatment. A criticism of the recommended definition could be: what if there is not a negative effect on the organization? It is virtually impossible to find an abused employee that is one hundred percent productive. The effect of abused employees will be felt by the organization in forms such as doing the bare minimum of effort on assigned tasks, coincidently absent from functions involving the toxic leader and additional stress at home. A toxic leader will never get above and beyond productivity from a quietly affected employee.

What are the Specific Characteristics of Toxic Leadership?

As with defining toxic leadership being a description, rather than a pure and true definition, there are descriptive actions and behaviors that if any one leader exhibits over an extended period of time or in an inappropriate situation, that person could and may be labeled toxic. "The Quick Wins Paradox" by Mark E. Van Buren and Todd Safferstone lists some of these characteristics:

1. "Focuses too heavily on the details."[7] Akin to micromanagement, and inability to see the big picture is detrimental to an organization. Leaders that get bogged down in minutiae, rarely share their ideas, thoughts, process or objectives with the team or their subordinates, leaving them guessing and confused. This is not a good state for subordinates or fellow team members to be in.

2. "Reacts negatively to criticism."[8] To be a successful leader one has to be able to intellectualize constructive criticism. A key component to combatting toxicity in leadership is putting a mirror on exhibited behaviors and seeking self-improvement. If a leader is unable to self-reflect or take in criticism he/she is unable to identify with which aspects of their leadership style require improvement. Another component of a leader that reacts poorly to criticism is that he/she could give off the attitude that they have "nothing to learn."[9]

3. "Intimidates others."[10] Commanding tones and threatening overtures do not bode well among subordinates or followers. This behavior leads to the leader being left to stand alone with no supporters or allies on his/her side.

37

4. "Jumps to hasty conclusions."[11] A failure to pause to thoroughly understand problems can result in solutions that do not meet requirements. Sometimes it is necessary to sit back and get a thorough understanding of a problem set before recommending a solution. Toxic leaders frequently frustrate members of an organization when they seemingly waste man-hours producing unnecessary work to an erroneous end.

5. "Micromanages direct reports."[12] This is another overly controlling behavior that causes leaders to do work that should be done by others. This is done for a multitude of reasons, one of which is a distorted rationale that they are helping the team and in a possibly self-centered manner, taking a heavier load than anyone else to appear as if they are carrying the team on their shoulders. This characteristic ties neatly with the military concept of a self-centered motivation contributing to toxicity.

"Toxic Leadership" by Colonel George E. Reed contributes three characteristic of a toxic leader for consideration:

1. An apparent lack of concern for the well-being of subordinates.[13]

2. A personality or interpersonal technique that negatively affects organizational climate.[14]

3. A conviction by subordinates that the leader is motivated primarily by self-interest[15]

Harsher characteristics are described by Bruce Heller, the author of "Toxic Boss Syndrome, What are the Causes and Cures?"

1. Emotional bullies.[16]

2. Treats employees coldly, even cruelly.[17]

3. They assign blame and take the credit for themselves.[18]

In "Toxic Leadership, Part Deux," Reed references a Harvard Professor's spin on "Bad Leadership" that includes incompetent, ridged, intemperate, callous, corrupt, insular and evil.[19] The issue with these characteristics is that just exhibiting one of these behaviors does not make a leader toxic. A leader could be incompetent and not very good at executing assigned tasks to standard and still be kind, considerate, outward thinking and morally good. Additionally, if a leader is corrupt, his/her leadership failure is not that he/she is toxic; it is that they are committing a Uniformed Code of Military Justice offense and their toxicity is a side issue.

Risky Business by Dr. Lynne McClure identifies toxic behaviors in civilian mangers:

1. Actor Behavior. These managers act out anger rather than discuss problems. They slam doors, sulk and make it clear they are angry, but refuse to talk about it. This behavior is extremely prevalent in military communities. It is an excepted practice and rarely called into question. The aspect of this behavior that brings this into the realm of toxicity for a military leader, is frequency. If the behavior happens daily, then perhaps that person can be considered toxic.

2. Fragmentor Behavior. These managers see no connection between what they do and the outcome, and take no responsibility for their behavior. This is typical of senior leaders that are not in touch with the realities of the people around them. There can be a direct correlation of fragmentors to leaders who fail to take a critical look at their behavior.

3. Me-First Behavior. These managers make decisions based on their own convenience. The issue with this behavior is that in the military a preponderance of

decisions made by leaders are based on their experience. If a leader has deployed into a combat zone, all combat related decisions are based on or are related to their personal deployments.

4. Mixed-Messenger Behavior. These managers present themselves one way, but their behavior does not match what they say. This is consistent with toxic tendencies but also comes very close to infringing on legal statutes and ethical standards of behavior. This is what led to trouble for Lieutenant Colonel Sasserman in Iraq in 2004.[20] He behaved as if there was nothing wrong and told his subordinates not to include damming information in the investigation.

5. Wooden-Stick Behavior. These managers are extremely rigid and controlling. Control is a staple of military life. It is the inability to remain flexible and adaptive that places a leader in the realm of toxic.

6. Escape-Artist Behavior. These managers do not deal with reality, often lying, or at the extreme, escaping through drugs or alcohol, another prevalent behavior within the military. Look at the high numbers of military personnel that abuse drugs and alcohol. There are untold numbers of functioning alcoholics. A less extreme example of not dealing with reality is leaders who do not see the blemishes of their organization, for example the leader who reads a command climate survey with negative comments and wishes away the bad parts to focus on the positive parts of the survey.

7. Shocker Behavior. These managers behave dramatically or extremely out of character. This is another behavior where frequency plays a role in deciding if it is toxic or not.

8. Stranger Behavior. These managers are extremely remote with poor social skills, and can become fixated on an idea or person. This behavior is not unique to the military or civilian sector. The impacts of poor social skills for a senior leader are more pronounced as he/she is forced to entertain at ceremonial events. Again, just having poor social skills does not make a leader toxic. Fixation alone does not make a leader toxic. A senior leader could be fixated with ensuring that the personnel in his/her care are being taken care of by the staff. Where the behavior becomes detrimental is when the fixation is on one person negatively or obsessively with an impact on the unit.

Do Toxic Leadership Characteristics Have
a Gender Component to Them?

No test or study needs to be conducted to determine if female leaders can exhibit the same negative/toxic or positive behaviors or traits as male leaders. The simple answer is yes, they can. The problem is that given all characteristics being equal, if females exhibit traditionally or culturally established masculine leadership characteristics, that female can be perceived in a less than favorable light.

Professor Alice Eagly and Professor Steven Karau, have extensively researched gender issues on the topic of leadership and published a study "Role Congruity Theory of Prejudice Towards Female Leaders."[21] The findings in their study suggest that perceived incongruity exists between the female gender role and leadership roles that leads to two forms of prejudice: (1) perceiving women less favorably than men as potential occupants of leadership roles; and (2) evaluating behavior that fills the prescriptions of a leader role less favorably when it is enacted by a woman.[22] The study asserts that the consequences of the prejudices are (1) attitudes that are less favorable towards female than male leaders; and (2) it is more difficult for women to become leaders and to achieve success in leadership positions.

It is soldiers such as SGM Teresa King who personify the impact of how other leaders negatively assess their seemingly masculine leadership style. SGM King, the first female Commandant of the Army Drill Sergeant School, resided in a predominantly male environment. King has the nickname of "Sergeant Major No Slack."[23] Her own words reflect a strong leader: "at the Direct Leadership Level I use Formal Leadership. I am a forward and future thinker, using expert power I am very skilled and proficient in my job."[24] With a reputation of being tough, she displayed the same behaviors as her male peers and counterparts. From her perspective she was just enforcing standards, in the eyes of her objectors she was being too tough, to the point of being toxic. She was publically accused of being toxic. There is no official charge for being toxic so she was charged with the "lost confidence in her ability to command."[25] This claim was investigated and subsequently dismissed. SGM King was officially acquitted of all charges against her, but that redemption is not featured in any of the numerous publications such as the *Army Times, Military Times*, or any blogs that condemned her as guilty before her innocence was proven. Less than reputable online publications such as MilitaryCurruption.com portrayed her as a toxic leader who needs to be kicked out of the Army. They have yet to publish any information on her redemption. The blogs have significance. Though not a scholarly source of credible information, these sites provide insight into the un-vetted thoughts and unabashed emotions of the members of the military. What is posted is assumed to be fact and credible by junior personnel. If such a site calls someone toxic, in the courts of public opinion he/she is labeled as such. The labeling is akin to what Dr.

Fallesen from CAL calls a "red herring that clouds the issues, and the label of toxic is too superficial"[26]

The 2004 *Encyclopedia of Leadership,* vol. *2,* defines "Gender Egalitarianism as the state or condition of minimizing gender role differences and promoting gender equity and equality." [27]The fact that a term with a definition exists acknowledges that there are gender differences. These gender differences exist and are not marginal conditions or anomalies. The effects of gender differences must be thoroughly understood by leadership of any organization.

The Alice H. Eagly and Mary C. Johannesen-Schmidt study in 1990 found that in a more traditional setting, where the male stereotype was more dominant, gender differences between men and women were more pronounced. The military is an undeniably male dominant environment which gives credence to the thought process of a distinction in leadership styles between male and female leaders.

Issues with the male dominance in military culture is not unique to the U.S. military. The British Army struggles with their culture as well. A 2005 newspaper article describes "the macho" culture in their training barracks as shared by female soldiers too, many of whom become obsessed with the need to trounce the boys. And despite their enthusiasm, "GI Janes" often become targets of abuse."[28] This is another example of the females trying to behave as the males do, and getting negative results.

The eyes of the perceiver play a crucial impact on how we judge female leaders. The findings by Becker, Ayman and Korabik in 2002 found the perceptions being evaluated originate from the subordinates of the leader.[29] In order to answer the question of, "are men and women behaving similarly or differently?" the answer may be contingent upon the eyes of the perceiver, who is influenced by his or her stereotypes,

expectations, and the social norms to which they have been.[30] In other words, if the male

subordinate grew up believing that the military is no place for a woman, or that the

proper place for a woman is at home, raising children, then his perceptions of how his

female military boss is performing will be skewed, most likely in a negative direction. If,

however he grew up with a pioneering female role model who excelled in a traditionally

male field, for example management, his perceptions of his female boss would be less

disagreeable.

What Can be Done to Effectively Identify, Address and Reduce Toxic Leadership?

> Several trends have emerged over the past decade . . . these trends have created an OE [operational environment] that is very dangerous, increasingly competitive, and always unpredictable. In response, our profession must embrace a culture of change and adaptation. We must think differently about how we develop leaders and how we organize, train, and equip our Soldiers and units.[31]

In 2011, the Army introduced the requirement to incorporate a comment about the

rated officer conducting a MSAF assessment. According to Army Regulation (AR) 623-3

Evaluations Reporting System dated 5 June 2012:

> Raters will verify if rated officers have initiated or completed a Multi-Source Assessment and Feedback (MSAF) in accordance with Army Regulation 350–1, Army Training and Leader Development, 18 December 2009, and will make a specific comment indicating such in part V, block b of the OER. The last statement in part V, block b of the OER will indicate "The rated officer has completed or initiated an Army multisource assessment and feedback as required by Army Regulation 350–1, Army Training and Leader Development, 18 December 2009," Rating officials are reminded that the MSAF is a self assessment tool. Although acknowledgment on the OER that a rated officer has initiated or completed an MSAF is required, the results of the MSAF will not be used as part of the formal evaluation. If a multi-source assessment has not been initiated or completed, no comment will be entered.[32]

This requirement may be an initial step to assist with combating toxic leadership. It is necessary to clarify that, at this time, there is no requirement to show anyone the results of the ratee's MSAF. It is strictly up to the individual to seek further assistance or counsel to improve any behaviors remarked in the MSAF. It is also necessary to clarify that the results of the MSAF are currently not taken into consideration for the official evaluation of officers' performance or leadership. This was validated by the Army Human Resources Command Commanding General, Major General Richard P. Mustion during a visit to the Command and General Staff College in October 2012. The Commanding General emphatically stated that "besides doing the 360 evaluation, no part of the Officer Evaluation Report is used to address or identify toxic leaders."

Amongst peers at the Command and General Staff College there is skepticism about future uses of the data generated from the MSAF, 360-degree Evaluation. This cynicism has led many to be wary about which peers, subordinates and supervisors they give their 360-degree Evaluation to. No one will send it to the people that have disagreed with them in the past or had negative interactions. If the evaluation is given to people who will only provide positive, approving feedback, the purpose of an honest assessment is defeated. According to Dr. Fallesen, in the future, Human Resources Command may direct who gets a 360-degree Evaluation by looking at an officer's records, picking personnel for the needed categories. The results will be evaluated or taken into consideration for candidates for brigade command. Therefore, the MSAF, the only tool that can address toxic leadership is not well liked.

Iin a YouTube video from February 2011, Annie McKee, founder of the Teleos

Leadership Institute, discusses toxic bosses. In this discussion, she best describes why we

should look at curbing toxic leadership:

> Emotions impact behavior, which impact results. Create an environment that is hopeful enthusiastic and a positive emotional environment. Emotions matter. Positive Leaders set a tone that has a sense of optimism and hope. Compassion is needed because, we want to serve the people around us, and help them succeed, and have the mindfulness, and the ability to stay grounded and effective in daily life.[33]

Source: Created by author using data from Headquarters, Department of the Army, Army Doctrine Publication 6-22, *Army Leadership* (Washington, DC: Government Printing Office, August 2012); Bernard M. Bass and Paul Steidlmeier, "Ethics, Character, and Authentic Transformational Leadership," Center for Leadership Studies, School of Management, Binghamton University, Binghamton, NY, 1998.

The study "An Exploration of Stereotypical Beliefs about Leadership Styles: Is Transformational Leadership a Route to Women's Promotion," found that "beliefs about sex differences in leadership style may be quite accurate."[34]

The study by Barbara Mandell and Shilpa Pherwani called "Relationship Between Emotional Intelligence and Transformational Leadership Style: A Gender Comparison," clearly asserts that "there is a predictive relationship between transformational leadership style and emotional intelligence."[35] "Research studies in leadership styles have established transformational leadership as one of the most effective ways of leading people."[36]

Another aspect that must be addressed is the disparity or dearth of examples of truly toxic leaders. The Navy publicly and swiftly fires underperforming and failing commanders. The *Navy Times* publishes for all to read why that commander was fired. Perhaps it is not necessary to publish faces and real names because we should have compassion for these people and their families; however, it is necessary for the field to know that the military is taking the claims of toxic leadership seriously and something is being done. Also public notice acts as a deterrent because deep down at our base level no one wants to be "that guy" [or girl]. "The real-life lessons and consequences,"[37] may go farther in curbing future toxic leadership, than solely teaching about good and positive leaders.

When asked, "What do you think can be done that is not being done to curtail toxic leadership?" SGM Teresa King stated, "hold all leaders accountable from Sergeants to Sergeants' Majors' and all officers as well, especially senior Officers.

Chapter Summary

This chapter discusses leadership styles that could be promoted by leader developers to neutralize the negative aspects of females that display masculine behavioral traits. The essence of the issue of gender in leadership is targeted to the discovered research that it is not what is being done that is looked upon with less favor; rather it is the mere fact of the gender of the executor of the behavior. Gender compounds leadership difficulties. When behavior is not in line with society's norms, it causes strife and an internal disconnect within individuals. It is this disconnect that causes females to be judged in an unfavorable light. Promoting a transformational leadership style could assist in providing a tangible tool when teaching leadership. SGM Teresa King is a plausible illustration of a female leader negotiating the toxic leadership label. Holding all leaders accountable is a step toward curbing toxic leadership.

---

[1]SGM Teresa King, e-mail interview by author, 12 November 2012.

[2]Headquarters, Department of the Army, Army Doctrine Publication (ADP) 6-22, *Army Leadership* (Washington, DC: Government Printing Office, August 2012).

[3]Jean Lipman-Blumen, "Toxic Leadership: When Grand Illusions Masquerade as Noble Visions."

[4]Kerfoot.

[5]Whicker, 11.

[6]Dr. Jon J. Fallesen, interview.

[7]Van Buren and Safferstone.

[8]Ibid.

[9]Ibid., 6.

[10]Ibid.

[11]Ibid.

[12]Ibid.

[13]Reed, "Toxic Leadership."

[14]Ibid.

[15]Ibid.

[16]Heller.

[17]Ibid.

[18]Ibid.

[19]Reed, "Toxic Leadership, Part Deux."

[20]Dexter Filkins, "Fall of the Warrior King" in L200, Leadership Applied Advance Sheet (Ft. Leavenworth, KS: Center for Army Leadership, Command and General Staff College, AY 2011-2012), 223.

[21]Eagly, Karau, and Makhijani, 125-145.

[22]Ibid.

[23]Joe Gould, "Army Suspends Drill Sergeant School Chief," *Army Times*, 13 December 2011, http://www.armytimes.com/news/2011/12/army-teresa-king-drill-sergeant-school-commandant-suspended-121311w/8fa2a67f9214c7994dfd823174014787 (accessed 8 July 2012).

[24]SGM Teresa King, interview.

[25]Joe Gould, "Army Times Prime," Gannett Government Media Corporation, http://www.armytimes.com/news/2012/05/army-drill-sergeant-commandant-king-reinstated-050412/8fa2a67f9214c7994dfd823174014787 (accessed 5 May 2012).

[26]Fallesen, interview.

[27]Goethals, Sorenson, and Burns, 578.

[28]Burke.

[29]Goethals, Sorenson, and Burns, 554.

[30]Ibid.

[31]General Martin E. Dempsey, "Driving Change Through a Campaign of Learning," *Army Magazine*.

[32]Headquarters, Department of the Army, Army Regulation (AR) 623-3, *Evaluation Reporting System* (Washington, DC: Government Printing Office, 5 June 2012), 30.

[33]Annie McKee, "Annie McKee Discusses Toxic Bosses," You Tube, http://www.youtube.com/watch?v=XNKJD5cuig4&feature=related (accessed 18 August 2012).

[34]Vinkenburg, 10-21, 12.

[35]Mandell and Pherwani, 401.

[36]Ibid., 398.

[37]"Fire Commanders Openly," *Army Times*, 25 June 2011, http://www.armytimes.com/community/opinion/army-fire-commanders-openly-editorial/ (accessed 29 August 2012).

CHAPTER 5

CONCLUSIONS AND RECOMMENDATIONS

Conclusions

The current definitions of toxic leadership are woefully insufficient to actually do anything about it. They are not tangible enough for the field to really understand it and prevent it. There is a cognitive dissonance that occurs when judging or evaluating female leaders. Because the military is predominantly a male institution, there is a role disconnect that causes female leaders to be subconsciously judged negatively. Adaptive and transformational leadership gives hope for existing toxic leaders and developing leaders.

Recommendations

Female leadership is grossly under researched. Perhaps because the leadership of the Armed Forces is unwilling to accept the notion that leadership is gendered. In this portion of the chapter, I propose a series of areas for future research.

A survey should be conducted on the effectiveness of the MSAF, 360-degree Evaluation. Explore whether or not officers are getting the desired benefits out of the program. Is it working the way it was intended to work? Is it providing a noticeable reduction in toxic leaders?

Conduct an indepth study on the question: "Are toxic leaders born or bred?" Is it the environment that can cause a leader to exude toxic mannerisms or is the toxicity pathological and an integrated part of the individual? The benefits of such a study would be to identify specific environments and situations that could trigger increased toxic behavior, and that acknowledgement could allow a leader to take necessary preventative action. An additional benefit of this study would be to send a message to the field that leadership can always be improved upon, and that the military is not going to discard you if you are prone to toxicity; but in fact the military will provided resources to rehabilitate. The notion of being invested goes a long way in boosting the optimistic outlook of leaders.

The relation of ethnicity to leadership should be explored. Are certain races or ethnic persuasions deemed better leaders based solely on their outward appearance, specifically skin color? The follow-on to this study can be: "Are there cultural gender differences that affect leadership within specific cultures." For example, if within Latin cultures, women are revered and deemed leaders of the community, then are Latin female military leaders stronger or better leaders than say Caucasian male and female leaders? The significance of this study would be that it could yield insight into how to better develop minority leaders. It could give Caucasian leaders areas for self-improvement that they were not aware of.

Another vein of research should be the leadership changes happen to female leaders as they progress through their career. General officers do not lead with the same mannerisms as they did as lieutenants. What personality and demeanor changes happen to leaders as they progress? Do they become hardened by the realities of the environment, and as a result, their leadership style is more harsh, aggressive and hard-nosed. Or does the confidence that can be afforded by a higher rank allow leaders to relax and taper their leadership style to a kinder, gentler temperament. The heart of this research could address what changes and what causes or triggers the changes. These changes can be evaluated because some changes in leadership style are necessary if you are going to be successful at adapting to different environments. The benefits of this line of research would be to bring to light what could happen to leaders. It could thwart the behaviors that make an innocent hearted lieutenant become a hardened toxic general.

Chapter Summary

Several areas of research are recommended for future study. These proposed research areas ranged from, evaluating the effectiveness of existing programs such as the 360-degree Evaluation, determining whether toxic leaders are born or bred, and learning what causes the temperament in a leader to change that makes them change their leadership style as they progress in rank. Insight into these areas of research would serve the Armed Forces well as they will have to focus on gender and how that area affects male leaders as opposed to how it affects female leaders. The added emphasis on gender will stop the erroneous, lazy and wishful notion that leadership does not have a gender component. This will lead to effective and impactful improvements in the development of leaders.

APPENDIX A

ORAL HISTORY QUESTIONS

Female Toxic Leadership Interview: Subject: Dr Jon J. Fallesen

Purpose: Qualitative literature of concepts and positions on female toxic leadership in support of MMAS thesis.

Method: In Person   Record: Notes

Qualifications:

1. Chief of Leadership Research, Assessment and Doctrine Division; Center For Army Leadership

2. Ph.D.

3. Technical Report 2011-13 Antecedents and consequences of toxic leadership in the U.S. Army: A two year review and recommended solutions.

Questions:

1. Why is it so difficult to define toxic leadership?

2. Currently there is no official DoD definition of toxic leadership. What is the hindrance to having an agreed upon Department of the Army or Department of Defense definition?

3. How can you address frequency of a behavior as it relates to being labeled toxic?

4. The ADRP 6-22 defines toxic leadership as :

Toxic Leadership is a combination of self-centered attributes, motivations and behaviors that have adverse effects on subordinates, the organization and mission performance. This leader lacks concern for others and the climate of the organization, which leads to short and long-term negative effects. The toxic leader operates with an inflated sense of self-worth and from acute self-interest. Toxic leaders consistently use dysfunctional behaviors to deceive, intimidate, coerce or unfairly punish others to get what they want for themselves.

How did you come up with these three features?

5. How do you reconcile the fact that all three elements are subjective and no objective measure is used in the description?

6. Do you believe that females are adversely affected by being labeled toxic leaders?

7. Is there any data to support your belief(s)?

8. Do you believe that the characteristics of toxic leaders can be judged differently if displayed by a female versus a male?

9. How does a senior leader become a toxic leader?

10. There has been an emphasis to address toxic leaders. The Army has introduced 360 assessments and the Navy publicly relieves toxic commanders. What do you think can be done that has not been implemented to curtail toxic leadership?

11. Can the promotion of a specific leadership style e.g adaptive leadership, provide a better framework to rehabilitate former toxic leaders and prevent the development of toxic behavior?

12. Public records rarely provide or describe the toxic behaviors or tangible details of why Commanders are being relieved beyond the statement of he/she was a toxic leader. Do you think that the lack of solid tangible examples of toxic behaviors is

a hindrance to curbing toxic behavior? Is toxic leadership too abstract to be

curbed?

Female Toxic Leadership Survey Subject: COL Dianna Robertson

Compiled, approved but not conducted.

Purpose: Qualitative literature of concepts and positions on female toxic leadership in support of MMAS thesis.

Method: Written   Record: Written

Qualifications:

1. Former 45th Sustainment Brigade Commander

2. Publically labeled as a toxic leader and removed from her brigade command position in Hawaii.

Proposed Questions:

1. How would you advise future female officers to conduct themselves in order to avoid being perceived as a toxic leader?

2. How would you describe your type of leadership style?

3. What was your previous awareness of toxic leadership?

4. Have you ever experienced a toxic leader?

5. Can you describe specific characteristics or action(s) that could be labeled as toxic?

6. Do you think that the military or Army is effectively addressing toxic leadership?

7. What are the problems with dealing with toxic leadership? Is it the message or how the message is being delivered?

8. In the delivery of the message, do you think that upcoming officers/senior non-commissioned officers can benefit by the publication of tangible post 9/11 examples of toxic leaders?

9. What do you think can be done that is not being done to curtail toxic leadership?

10. Do you believe that females are more adversely affected by being labeled toxic leaders?

11. Is there any data to support your belief(s)?

12. Do you believe that the characteristic of toxic leaders can be judged differently if displayed by a female versus a male?

13. What could be some teachable moments that could be redeemed from your experience?

Female Toxic Leadership Interview Subject: CSM Teresa King

Purpose: Qualitative literature of concepts and positions on female toxic leadership in support of MMAS thesis.

Method: Written   Record: Written

Qualifications:

- The first female commandant of the Army Drill Sergeants School at Fort Jackson, South Carolina.

- Publically accused of being a toxic leader; subsequently exonerated of all charges.

    1. How would you advise future female Soldiers to conduct themselves in order to avoid being perceived as a toxic leader?

    2. How would you describe your type of leadership style?

    3. What was your previous awareness of toxic leadership?

    4. Have you ever experienced a toxic leader?

    5. Can you describe specific characteristics or action(s) that could be labeled as toxic?

    6. Do you think that the military or Army is effectively addressing toxic leadership?

    7. What are the problems with dealing with toxic leadership? Is it the message or how the message is being delivered?

    8. In the delivery of the message, do you think that upcoming officers/senior non-commissioned officers can benefit by the publication of tangible post 9/11 examples of toxic leaders?

9. What do you think can be done that is not being done to curtail toxic leadership?

10. Do you believe that females are more adversely affected by being labeled toxic leaders?

11. Is there any data to support your belief(s)?

12. Do you believe that the characteristic of toxic leaders can be judged differently if displayed by a female versus a male?

13. What could be some teachable moments that could be redeemed from your experience?

APPENDIX B

CONSENT AND USE AGREEMENT FOR ORAL HISTORY MATERIALS

CONSENT AND USE AGREEMENT FOR ORAL HISTORY MATERIALS

You have the right to choose whether or not you will participate in this oral history interview, and once you begin you may cease participating at any time without penalty. The anticipated risk to you in participating is negligible and no direct personal benefit has been offered for your participation. If you have questions about this research study, please contact the student at: (254) 702-2748 or Dr. Robert F. Baumann, Director of Graduate Degree Programs, at (913) 684-2742.

To: Director, Graduate Degree Programs
Room 4508, Lewis & Clark Center
U.S. Army Command and General Staff College

1. I, Dr. Jon Fallsen participated in a written oral history interview conducted by MAJ Naomi Carrington, a graduate student in the Master of Military Art and Science Degree Program, on the following date [s]: 22 October 2012 concerning the following topic: Female Toxic Leadership.

2. I understand that the written recording [s] and any transcript resulting from this oral history will belong to the U.S. Government to be used in any manner deemed in the best interests of the Command and General Staff College or the U.S. Army, in accordance with guidelines posted by the Director, Graduate Degree Programs and the Center for Military History. I also understand that subject to security classification restrictions I will be provided with a copy of the recording for my professional records. In addition, prior to the publication of any complete edited transcript of this oral history, I will be afforded an opportunity to verify its accuracy.

3. I hereby expressly and voluntarily relinquish all rights and interests in the written recording [s] with the following caveat:

_____ None _____ Other: _____

I understand that my participation in this oral history interview is voluntary and I may stop participating at any time without explanation or penalty. I understand that the tapes and transcripts resulting from this oral history may be subject to the Freedom of Information Act, and therefore, may be releasable to the public contrary to my wishes. I further understand that, within the limits of the law, the U.S. Army will attempt to honor the restrictions I have requested to be placed on these materials.

Dr. Jon Fallsen   30 OCT 2012
_____   _____   _____
Name of Interviewee   Signature   Date

                                                              30 OCT 2012
_____   _____   _____
Accepted on Behalf of the Army by   Signature   Date
MAJ Naomi Carrington

CONSENT AND USE AGREEMENT FOR ORAL HISTORY MATERIALS

You have the right to choose whether or not you will participate in this oral history interview, and once you begin you may cease participating at any time without penalty. The anticipated risk to you in participating is negligible and no direct personal benefit has been offered for your participation. If you have questions about this research study, please contact the student at: (254) 702-2748 or Dr. Robert F. Baumann, Director of Graduate Degree Programs, at (913) 684-2742.

To: Director, Graduate Degree Programs
Room 4508, Lewis & Clark Center
U.S. Army Command and General Staff College

1. I, SGM Teresa L. King, participated in a written oral history interview conducted by MAJ Naomi

Carrington, a graduate student in the Master of Military Art and Science Degree Program, on the

following date [s]: 22 October 2012 concerning the following topic: Female Toxic Leadership.

2. I understand that the written recording [s] and any transcript resulting from this oral history will belong to the U.S. Government to be used in any manner deemed in the best interests of the Command and General Staff College or the U.S. Army, in accordance with guidelines posted by the Director, Graduate Degree Programs and the Center for Military History. I also understand that subject to security classification restrictions I will be provided with a copy of the recording for my professional records. In addition, prior to the publication of any complete edited transcript of this oral history, I will be afforded an opportunity to verify its accuracy.

3. I hereby expressly and voluntarily relinquish all rights and interests in the written recording [s] with the following caveat:

____X__ None   _____ Other: _____

I understand that my participation in this oral history interview is voluntary and I may stop participating at any time without explanation or penalty. I understand that the tapes and transcripts resulting from this oral history may be subject to the Freedom of Information Act, and therefore, may be releasable to the public contrary to my wishes. I further understand that, within the limits of the law, the U.S. Army will attempt to honor the restrictions I have requested to be placed on these materials.

SGM Teresa L. King

_____   _____
Name of Interviewee   Signature   Date   12 Nov 12

_____   _____
Accepted on Behalf of the Army by   Signature   Date   16 NOV 12
MAJ Naomi Carrington

APPENDIX C

INTERVIEW WITH CSM TERESA KING

Response to Female Toxic Leader Interview: CSM Teresa King

1. Describe the specific characteristics or action(s) that you were accused of to be labeled a toxic leader?

The specific characteristic or action was unclear. There was a Climate assessment conducted by the TRADOC IG which I was never briefed on. All complaints and no facts were taken from an unfair proportion of the cadre and students in the school. Soldiers complained of working too many hours, and me being a micromanager. Most cadres were on Drill Sergeant Duty, which called for the extraordinary hours. The part about micromanager was as a CSM should, I checked on training since the Commandant was responsible by TRADOC 350-16 to execute the DSS Program of Instruction. In addition, I observed Physical Fitness daily at 0430, ranges, field training, live fires, and during their classes both inside and outside. This is what a Command Sergeant Major and leader is supposed to do. I should mention that technically I was not suspended for Toxic Leadership because it was removed from the formal investigation results by the investigating officer.

2. How would you describe your type of leadership style?

At the Direct Leadership Level I use Formal Leadership. I am a forward and future thinker, using expert power I am very skilled and proficient in my job. At the same time I have great compassion and care for Soldiers and all people. The Army Values are at my

63

core and I use the leader principles of Jesus Christ. Hard but fair and insist all Soldiers are respected and meet and maintain the standard. My door is always open staying late or arriving early to hear a Soldier. I lead from the front. For example when it is time to weigh in, take APFT or group and zero with a weapon me and my senior leaders are first in line.

3. What was your previous awareness of toxic leadership?

My awareness of Toxic Leadership was leaders who were self-serving, who show and demonstrate a lack of concern for others, does not set the example, unethical, violated Army Values and UCMJ.

4. Have you ever experienced a toxic leader?

Yes I have experienced a toxic leader. I was complaining to my chain of command about this leader's toxicity when I came under investigation as a result of that.

5. Do you think that the military or Army is effectively addressing toxic leadership ?

No, I do not believe Soldiers understand the meaning of Toxic Leadership other than what's negatively planted by leaders who are using it for personal gain.

6. What are the problems with dealing with toxic leadership? Is it the message or how the message is being delivered.?

It is not well defined throughout the Army. Toxic Leadership must be defined at a level where all soldiers can understand it. It is routinely confused with leaders enforcing standards and used by subordinates to escape being held accountable.

7. In the delivery of the message, do you think that upcoming officers/senior non-commissioned officers can benefit by the publication of tangible post 9/11 examples of toxic leaders?

I think well defined examples will be beneficiary, but not exclusively those published. However, more announcements and holding all leaders accountable for what they do and don't do would be most effective in eradicating Toxic Leadership. A return to doctrine by all would be a 105 percent way of eradicating toxic leadership.

8. What do you think can be done that is not being done to curtail toxic leadership?

Hold all leaders accountable from Sergeants to Sergeant Majors and all officers as well, especially senior officers.

9. How would you advise future female leaders to conduct themselves in order to avoid being perceived as a toxic leader?

Female Leaders who are proficient and strong will unfortunately be labeled toxic. I would advise them to strictly use Army regulations as a guide, be strong and pray because they are sure to come under fire at some point for enforcing standards or for doing their job.

10. What could be some teachable moments that could be redeemed from your experiences?

When you select a female to do something that's never been done, ensure there is continuous support from the Top Army leaders.

11. Do you believe that females are more adversely affected by being labeled toxic leaders?

Yes, strong female leaders who are strong and can lead from the front, are more adversely being labeled toxic. Many male peers are and female soldiers have not adopted the Army position on this. They secretly gossip, complain and unobjectively make ludicrous comments and complaints which hold no validity because they simply disagree with the decision to place a female in a male dominated position.

12. Is there any data to support your belief(s)?

Yes, there are many who have told me their story and are afraid to speak up. They fear reprisal and career assassination.

13. Do you believe that the characteristics of toxic leaders can be judged differently if displayed by a female versus a male?

Absolutely! If I were a male there would have never been an investigated. I was suspended without even a reason, conversation or counseling.

BIBLIOGRAPHY

Books

Bonaparte, Napoleon. Quoted in Byron Farwell. *Encyclopedia of 19th Century Land Warfare: An Illustrated World View*. New York, NY: W. W. Norton & Company, 2001.

Drucker, Peter. *Management Challenges for the 21st Century*. New York, NY: Harper Collins, 1999.

Given, Lisa M. *The Sage Encyclopedia of Qualitative Research Methods*. Los Angeles, CA: Sage Publications, 2008.

Goethals, George R., Georgia J. Sorenson, and MacGregor Burns. *Encyclopedia of Leadership*. Vol. 2. Thousand Oaks, CA: Sage, 2004.

Kellerman, Barbara. *Bad Leadership, What it is, How it Happens and Why it Matters*. Boston, MA: Harvard Business School, 2004.

Lipman-Blumen, Jean. *The Allure of Toxic Leaders*. New York, NY: Oxford University Press, 2005.

Northhouse, Peter G. *Leadership: Theory and Practice*. 5th ed. India: Sage, 2011.

Price, Terry L. *Understanding Ethical Failures in Leadership*. New York, NY: Cambridge University Press, 2006.

Warneka, Timothy H. *Leading People the Black Belt Way, Conquering the Five Core Problems Facing Leaders Today*. Cleveland, OH: Asogomi Publishing International, 2006.

Whicker, Marcia Lynn. *Toxic Leaders; When Organizations Go Bad*. Westport, CT: Quorm Books, 1996.

Williams, Christopher. *Leadership Accountability in a Globalizing World*. New York, NY: Palgrave Macmillian, 2006.

Government Documents

Headquarters, Department of the Army. Army Doctrine Publication (ADP) 6-22, *Army Leadership*. Washington, DC: Government Printing Office, August 2012.

———. Army Doctrine Reference Publication (ADRP) 6-22, *Army Leadership*. Washington, DC: Government Printing Office, August 2012.

———. Army Regulation (AR) 623-3, *Evaluation Reporting System*. Washington, DC: Government Printing Office, 5 June 2012.

———. Field Manual (FM) 6-22, *Army Leadership*. Washington, DC: Government Printing Office, 12 October 2006.

Steele, Dr. John P. *CASAL: Army Leaders' Perceptions of Army Leaders and Army Leadership Practices* Special Report 2011-1. Ft. Leavenworth, KS: Center for Army Leadership, June 2011.

Internet Sources

2012 HubPages Inc. http://thejeffriestube.hubpages.com/hub/Admiral-Chester-Nimitz-Savior-of-the-Pacific-Fleet (accessed 4 May 2012).

About.com. "US Military Promotions." http://usmilitary.about.com/od/promotions /l/blofficerprom.htm (accessed 17 June 2012).

The American Academy of Achievement. http://www.achievement.org/autodoc/ page/sch0int-5 (accessed 5 May 2012).

Beck, Cheryl T. "They Lived Experience of Postpartum Depression: A Phenomenological Study." *Nursing Research*, 41, no. 3 (May-June 1992): 166-170. http://psycnet.apa.org/psycinfo/1992-43176-001 (accessed 3 December 2012).

Burke, Joanna. "From Surrey to Basra, Abuse is a Fact of British Army Life." *The Guardian*, 26 February 2005. http://www.guardian.co.uk/uk/2005/feb/26/ military.iraq/print (accessed 29 August 2012).

Capilanou University. http://www2.capilanou.ca/programs/psychology/students/ research/phenom.html (accessed 5 August 2012).

Dempsey, General Martin E. "Letter to the Force." DOD Live.mil, 1 October 2011. http://www.dodlive.mil/index.php/2011/10/general-dempseys-letter-to-the-joint-force/ (accessed 22 July 2012).

Dulcinea Media Inc. "On this Day." http://www.findingdulcinea.com/news/on-this-day/July-August-08/On-this-Day--General-Patton-Shocks-Public-by-Slapping-Crying-Soldier.html (accessed 4 May 2012).

Eagly, Alice H., Steven J. Karau, and Mona G. Makhijani. Abstract from "Gender and the Effectiveness of Leaders: A Meta-Analysis," *Psychological Bulletin* 117, no. 1 (1995):125-145, http://www.ncbi.nlm.nih.gov/pubmed/12088246 (accessed 5 September 2012).

"Fire Commanders Openly," *Army Times*, 25 June 2011, http://www.armytimes.com/community/opinion/army-fire-commanders-openly-editorial/ (accessed 29 August 2012).

Gould, Joe. "Army Suspends Drill Sergeant School Chief." *Army Times*, 13 December 2011. http://www.armytimes.com/news/2011/12/army-teresa-king-drill-sergeant-school-commandant-suspended-121311w/8fa2a67f9214c7994dfd823174014787 (accessed 8 July 2012).

———. "Army Times Prime News." *Army Times*. http://www.armytimes.com/news/2012/05/army-drill-sergeant-commandant-king-reinstated-050412/8fa2a67f9214c7994dfd823174014787 (accessed 7 August 2012).

Hani, Dr. "Empirical Research." Experiment Resources, 2009. http://www.experiment-resources.com/empirical-research.html (accessed 18 August 2012).

Hay, Ian. "Transformational Leadership: Characteristics and Criticisms." School of Geography, Population and Environmental Management, Flinders University. http://www.leadingtoday.org/weleadinlearning/transformationalleadership.htm (accessed 4 September 2012).

MacDonald, Glenn, MAJ USAR (RET). Editor-n-Chief. "Military Corruption." http://www.militarycorruption.com/ (accessed 5 September 2012).

McClure, Dr. Lynn F. *Risky Business.* Binghamton, NY: Haworth, 1996. http://books.google.com/books?id=KUSUcetrUBQC&dq=Lynne+Mcclure+Risky+Business&lr=&source=gbs_navlinks_s (accessed 6 June 2012).

McKee, Annie McKee. "Annie McKee Discusses Toxic Bosses." You Tube. http://www.youtube.com/watch?v=XNKJD5cuig4&feature=related (accessed 18 August 2012).

Staniland, Paul. "States, Insurgents, and Wartime Political Orders." *Perspectives on Politics* 10 (2012): 243-264. http://journals.cambridge.org/action/displayAbstract?fromPage=online&aid=8593713 (accessed 13 September 2012).

Top Tenz. "2012 Top 10 Lists." http://www.toptenz.net/top-10-worst-military-leaders-in-history.php (accessed 4 May 2012).

UK. "CSM Teresa King." http://www.militarycorruption.com/csmteresaking.htm (accessed 8 July 2012).

The Ulyssses S. Grant Homepage. http://www.granthomepage.com/grantgeneral.htm (accessed 4 May 2012).

University of California Press. http://publishing.cdlib.org/ucpressebooks/view?docId=
ft0k40037v&chunk.id=d0e2943&toc.depth=100&brand=eschol (accessed 12
August 2012).

U.S. Census Bureau, Newsroom. "Women's History Month: March 2012." http://www.
census.gov/newsroom/releases/archives/facts_for_features_special_editions/cb12-
ff05.html (accessed 29 June 2012).

Van Buren, Mark E., and Todd Safferstone. "The Quick Wins Paradox." *Harvard
Business Review* (January 2009): 55. http://hbr.org/2009/01/the-quick-wins-
paradox/ar/1 (accessed 12 June 2012).

Journals/Periodicals

Athanasopouos, CPT George J. "Improving Toxic Leadership." *Army Magazine.*

Boddy, Clive R. "Corporate Psychopaths, Bullying and Unfair Supervision in the
Workplace." *Journal of Business Ethics* (2011): 367-379.

Dempsey, General Martin E. "Driving Change Through a Campaign of Learning." *Army
Magazine* (October 2010).

Eagly, Alice H., and Mary C. Johannesen-Schmidt. "The Leadership Styles of Women
and Men." *Journal of Social Issues* (2001): 781-797.

Eagly, Alice H., Mary C. Johannesen-Schmidt, and Marloes L. van Engen.
"Transformational, Transactional, and Laissez-Faire Leadership Styles."
Psychological Bulletin 129, no. 4 (2003): 569-591.

Eagly, Alice H., and Steven J. Karau. "Role Congruity Theory of Prejudice Towards
Female Leaders. *Psychology Review* 109, no. 3 (July 2002): 573-598.

Eagly, Alice H., Steven J. Karau, and Mona G. Makhijani. "Gender and the Effeciviness
of Leaders: A Meta-Analysis." *Psychlogical Bulletin* 117, no. 1 (1995): 125-145.

Eagly, Alice H., and Valerie J. Steffen. "Gender Stereotypes Stem From the Distribution
of Women and Men Into Social Roles." *Journal of Personality and Social
Psychology* 45, no. 4 (1984): 735-754.

Gould Joe. "Circus of Mistakes." *Army Times,* 22 October 2012.

Heller, Bruce. "Toxic Boss Syndrome, What are the Causes and Cures?" *Sales and
Service Excellence* (June 2010): 15.

Kerfoot, Karlene M. "Leadership, Civility and the 'No Jerks' Rule." *Urologic Nursing*
28, no. 2 (April 2008): 149.

Lipman-Blumen, Jean. "Toxic Leadership: When Grand Illusions Masquerade as Noble Visions." *Leader to Leader* (Spring 2005): 29-36.

Mandell, Barbara, and Shilpa Pherwani. "Relationship Between Emotional Intelligence & Transformational Leadership Style." *Journal of Business and Psychology* 17, no 3 (Spring 2003).

Reed, COL George E. "Toxic Leadership." *Military Review* (July-August 2004): 67-71.

———. "Toxic Leadership, Part Deux." *Military Review* (November 2010): 58-64.

Springer. "Ethical Leadership." *Journal of Business Ethics* (2009): 3.

Tan, Michelle, and Joe Gould. "Army Wants to Rid Top Ranks of Toxic Leaders." *Army Times*, 31 July 2011. http://www.armytimes.com/news/2011/07/army-wants-to-rid-ranks-of-toxic-commanders-73111w/ (accessed 10 July 2012).

Vinkenburg, C. J. "An Exploration of Stereotypical Beliefs about Leadership Styles: Is Transformational Leadership a Route to Women's Promotion." *The Leadership Quarterly International Journal of Political Social and Behavioral Science*, 22 (2011): 10-21.

Yoder, J. D. "Making Leadership Work More Effectively for Women." *Journal of Social Issues* 57, no. 5 (2001): 815-828.

Other Sources

Bass, Bernard M., and Paul Steidlmeier. "Ethics, Character, and Authentic Transformational Leadership." Center for Leadership Studies, School of Management, Binghamton University, Binghamton, NY, 1998.

Fallesen, Dr. Jon J. Interview with author. Ft. Leavenworth, KS, 30 October 2012.

Filkins, Dexter. "Fall of the Warrior King." In L200, Leadership Applied Advance Sheet. Ft. Leavenworth, KS: Center for Army Leadership, Command and General Staff College, AY 2011-2012.

King, SGM Teresa. E-mail interview by author. 12 November 2012.